ínspirations

TIN CRAFTS

Over 20 creative projects for the home

ínspirations

TIN CRAFTS

Over 20 creative projects for the home

MARY MAGUIRE

PHOTOGRAPHY BY MICHELLE GARRETT

LORENZ BOOKS

First published in 1999 by Lorenz Books

Lorenz Books is an imprint of
Anness Publishing Limited
Hermes House
88–89 Blackfriars Road
London SE1 8HA

Published in the USA by Lorenz Books,
Anness Publishing Inc., 27 West 20th Street,
New York, NY 10011; (800) 354-9657

This edition distributed in Canada by Raincoast Books,
8680 Cambie Street, Vancouver, British Columbia V6P 6M9

A CIP catalogue record for this book is available from the British Library.

ISBN 1 85967 886 6

Publisher: Joanna Lorenz
Project Editor: Emma Clegg
Photographer: Michelle Garrett
Step Photographer: Rodney Forte
Designer: Lilian Lindblom
Illustrators: Madeleine David and Vana Haggerty
Production: Don Campaniello

Printed and bound in Hong Kong/China

1 3 5 7 9 10 8 6 4 2

Publisher's Note
The author and publishers have made every effort to ensure that all the instructions in this book are accurate and safe, and therefore cannot
accept liability for any resulting injury, damage or loss to persons or property however it may arise.

Acknowledgements
The publishers and author would like to thank the following artists for the beautiful projects photographed in this book:
Penny Boylan: String Dispenser, Shimmering Temple, Musical Scarecrow and Embossed Greetings Cards;
Marion Elliot: Leaf Curtain-edging and Moorish Flower Blind; Andrew Gillmore: Punched-panel Wall Cabinet, Hammered Weather Vane,
Classic Mailbox and Metal-faced Drawers; Deborah Schneebeli-Morrell: Repoussé Frame, Christmas Birds and Beer-can Candle Sconce.
The clock mechanism for the Contemporary Clock was kindly supplied by Bude Time Enterprises Ltd, Higher Wharf, Bude, Cornwall
EX23 8LW (tel: 01288 342832). A big thank you also to Michelle Garrett for her project photographs,
to Rodney Forte for the step-by-step photography and to Emma Clegg for her organization.

CONTENTS

INTRODUCTION

Creating wonderful accessories and decorations out of tin has the same attraction as the craft of papier-mâché, in that it can recycle and transform quite ordinary existing materials. It is possible to experiment with metal foil in different thicknesses and with different qualities. But you can also make original items out of everyday objects that you might not otherwise think of using that can be found in your kitchen cupboard, such as baking tins and cake moulds or throwaway materials such as cans and tins.

The other great attraction is that no complex or expensive specialist tools are needed – just a steady hand. Start by turning out your cupboard or pay a visit to your local hardware store and you will be able to make a simple candle sconce bolted together from two petit four tins or a clock from cake moulds. Further on you will discover how to emboss tin foil to create memorable greeting cards, or even simpler still, using a ready-made stencil as your design. Once you have started working through the many simple ideas featured here, I am sure that you will not be able to stop yourself moving on to the more ambitious ones such as the Musical Scarecrow out of cans, the Mexican Mirror frame and the Moorish Flower Blind.

Projects start with those for the beginner and move on to larger projects as you gain confidence. Each one features clear step-by-step photography and includes details of every material and piece of equipment, so that everything will be readily available. In addition, templates are included at the back of the book so you can re-create the designs exactly. Just start saving those tin cans now and you will then be in a position to fill your home with outstanding, creative ideas that everyone will admire.

Deborah Barker

HEART CANDLE SCONCE

The beauty of this project lies in its sheer simplicity; two patisserie (baking) tins have been turned into a delightful wall decoration by the cunning use of an ordinary metal angle bracket. The heart will reflect the flame of a small candle or night-light.

YOU WILL NEED
6-holed angle bracket
7.5 cm/3 in heart-shaped cake tin
7.5 cm/3 in diameter circular cake tin
permanent marker
drill
2 nuts and bolts
spanner (wrench)
rawl plugs (optional)
screwdriver
screw (optional)
candle or night-light

1 Lay the angle bracket against the back of each cake tin – the heart tin positioned vertically and the circular tin as the base. Make a mark through the holes in the bracket with a permanent marker.

2 Drill through the cake tins as marked. Note that the photograph is styled for clarity – the drill would be perpendicular to the object which would be taped and clamped (see Basic Techniques).

3 Use nuts and bolts to join the tins to the bracket. Predrill and plug the wall, and then screw through the hole in the heart and the bracket into the wall behind. Add the candle to complete the project.

EMBOSSED HEART

*Make this exquisite decoration to personalize a special gift for a loved one. Here it is used
as the finishing touch on a pretty album. Metal stencils come in many designs
and make embossing foil simple, so this is an easy project to start with.*

YOU WILL NEED
small, pointed scissors
0.1 mm/½₅₀ in pewter or aluminium foil
metal stencil
double-sided carpet tape
protective pad
double-ended embossing stylus
sewing needle (optional)
pinking shears or deckle-edged scissors (optional)
album, box or card

1 Cut out a piece of pewter or aluminium foil
large enough to take the metal stencil plus a
small border all round it. Secure the stencil on to the
foil with a couple of small tabs of double-sided carpet
tape, making sure they do not cover any of the holes.
Lay the foil on a protective pad. Use the thin end of
the embossing stylus to outline the stencil.

2 Indent the pattern by drawing the outlines of the
shapes then rubbing over the whole area. Use the
thin end for small shapes, and the wide end for large
areas. For shapes too small for the stylus, use the
blunt end of a needle.

3 Remove the stencil and continue to work on the image to refine the definition of the motifs.

4 Cover the indented side of the foil with double-sided carpet tape, then turn the foil over and cut out the heart. Use small, pointed scissors to cut just outside the indented outline or, for a decorative border, use pinking shears.

5 Remove the adhesive backing and stick the tin motif on to the album, box or card. To make it even more secure, work the stylus around the edge pressing in between the raised dots.

Above: This classic heart shape is ideal for mounting on a special album to protect favourite photographs or letters

CONTEMPORARY CLOCK

Minimalist detail and smooth contours give this clock a sophisticated look of industrial chic.
The clock is constructed simply from two ordinary aluminium ring moulds so that the inner
mould neatly encloses the clock movement.

YOU WILL NEED
2 aluminium ring moulds
drill
clock mechanism with extra long shank
saucer or plate
paper
pencil
scissors
strong glue
4 square 1 cm/½in nuts
double-sided adhesive pads

1 Choose two ring moulds that fit well together. Drill a hole through the centre of the smaller mould to take the shank for the clock hands.

2 Insert the clock mechanism and screw in place. Make sure the hands will fit inside the rim of the small mould.

3 Cut out a circle of paper by tracing around a
saucer which is about the size of the highest point
of the large mould. Fold it carefully into quarters,
unfold it and lay it on top of the mould. Make a light
pencil mark on the mould at each quarter line.

4 Using strong glue, carefully fix a square nut at
each quarter mark of the clock.

5 Set the hands at 12 o'clock
and fix the small mould into
the larger one using adhesive
pads, aligning the hands with one
of the quarter marks.

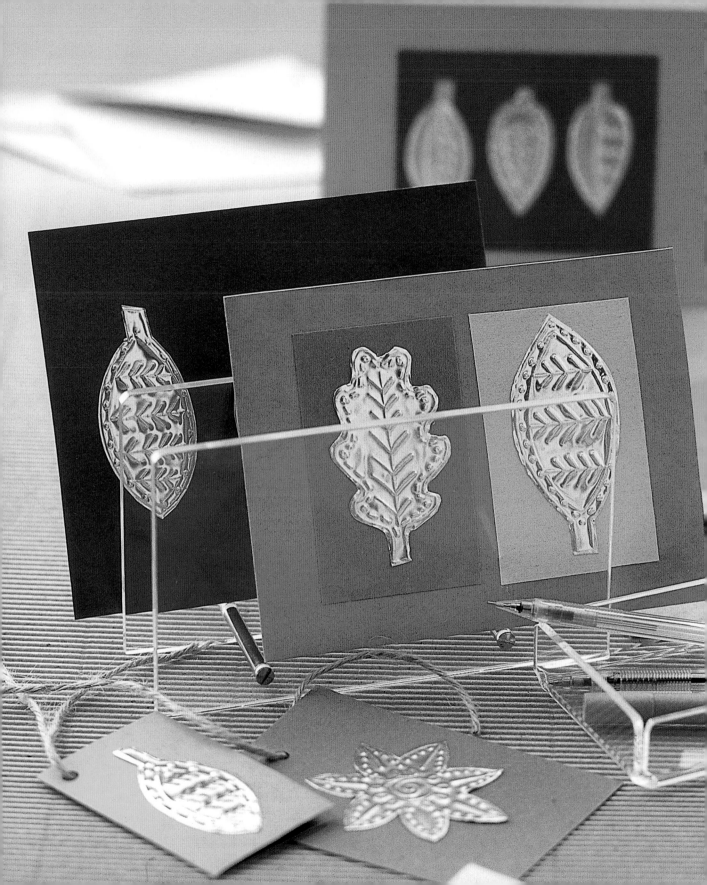

EMBOSSED GREETINGS CARDS

*Using small scraps of heavy-gauge aluminium foil you can quickly and easily make
your own glittering greetings cards, building up the designs on toned shades of plain card.
Use single motifs to make stylish, matching gift tags.*

YOU WILL NEED
tracing paper
pencil
adhesive tape
0.1 mm/¹⁄₂₅₀ in aluminium foil
protective pad
dried-out ball-point pen
small, pointed scissors
coloured card (cardboard)
double-sided carpet tape or all-purpose glue
hole punch
ribbon or braid

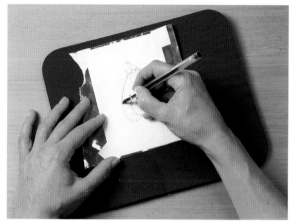

1 Trace a template from the back of the book and
tape it to a piece of aluminium foil. Rest the
foil on a protective pad and draw over the lines of
the tracing with a dried-out ball-point pen to transfer
the design.

2 Remove the tracing and redraw the lines to
make the embossing more pronounced.

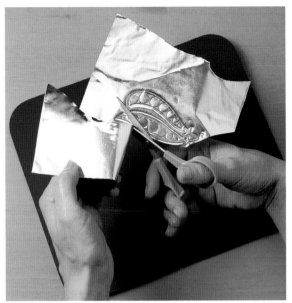

3 Turn the foil over and cut around the motif with small, pointed scissors, leaving a very narrow margin all around the edge.

4 Stick the motif on to a piece of coloured card (cardboard) using either double-sided carpet tape or all-purpose glue.

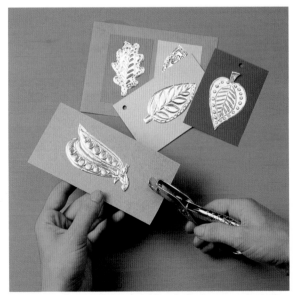

5 To make a gift tag punch a hole in one edge of the card for ribbon or braid. For larger greetings cards, glue a variety of motifs on card in contrasting colours before mounting them on folded card.

Above: The most effective motifs are usually the simplest, particularly for a small-scale item such as this gift tag

REPOUSSÉ FRAME

This delicate foil frame is decorated using the repoussé (embossing) technique, in which the raised design is created by impressing the back of the metal. Use the template to cut a foam-board backing for your picture, then stick the frame to the front.

YOU WILL NEED
tracing paper
pencil
0.1 mm/$\frac{1}{250}$ in copper foil
adhesive tape
protective pad
dried-out ball-point pen
ruler
dressmaker's tracing wheel
small, pointed scissors
foam board
double-sided carpet tape or all-purpose glue

1 Trace the template from the back of the book and attach the tracing paper to a sheet of copper foil using adhesive tape. Rest the foil on a protective pad and transfer the design by drawing lightly over the lines with a dried-out ball-point pen. Use a ruler for the straight lines.

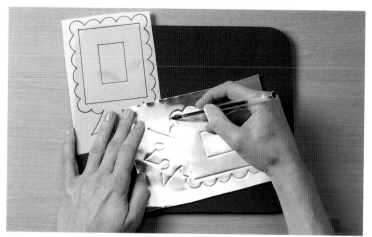

2 Remove the tracing paper and then use the ball-point pen to press more firmly over the lightly drawn lines. Remember to use an even pressure throughout the whole piece to make the marks consistent.

3 Use a tracing wheel to outline the outer and inner edges and add the detail to the crown.

4 Use the ball-point pen to draw the crossed lines between the tracing wheel outlines. Then draw a star in each scallop around the edge by making four crossed lines.

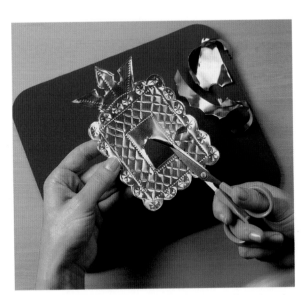

5 When the design is complete, use small, pointed scissors to cut carefully around the frame. To cut out the central section, pierce the metal in the centre with the point of the scissors, and then cut to the edge of the opening.

6 Use the template to cut out a sheet of foam board in the shape of the frame. Mount your picture in the centre of the foam board and attach the metal frame to the foam board, embossed side down, with double-sided carpet tape or all-purpose glue.

SCROLLWORK DOORSTOP

Pewter shim is easy to emboss, whether you use freestyle curlicues or a more formal pattern.
A wooden block is wrapped like a parcel with the embossed pewter to make this doorstop,
which could also be used as an elegant book-end.

YOU WILL NEED

pewter shim, 39.5 x 40 cm/15 x 15½ in
protective pad
permanent marker
ruler
embossing stylus
dried-out ball-point pen
pencil
lollipop (Popsicle) stick
wooden block, 19 x 9 x 9 cm/7½ x 3½ x 3½ in
2 metal washers, 4 cm/1½ in diameter
hammer
2 roofing nails

1 Lay the pewter shim on a protective pad and, following the template from the back of the book, use a permanent marker and ruler to draw the fold lines on the metal. Using a dried-out ball-point pen, score a line 3 mm/⅛ in in from one end and fold over. Score along all the solid marked lines. Turn the pewter over and score the remaining dotted lines.

2 Turn the sheet back again and use a permanent marker pen to draw the pattern freehand on the areas shown on the template.

3 Score the pattern on the pewter with a stylus or pencil. Use a lollipop (Popsicle) stick end for thick lines and a ball-point pen for fine ones.

4 Turn the sheet over and complete the design by indenting tiny dots around the lines using the stylus or dried-out ball-point pen.

5 Wrap the pewter around the wooden block, allowing the neatened, folded edge to overlap the other edge.

6 Fold along the scored lines and wrap up the block as if it were a present.

▶

7 Place a metal washer centrally on the end of the block and hammer a roofing nail through it to secure the pewter and give it interesting detail. Repeat at the other end of the block.

MUSICAL SCARECROW

*This lady scarecrow will bring a note of whimsy to your vegetable garden, but she will
also protect your crops from marauding birds by rattling and jingling in the breeze.
Look in the supermarket for colourful printed aluminium cans to use.*

YOU WILL NEED
assorted aluminium drinks (soda) cans
scissors
paper
pencil
adhesive tape
tape measure
madeleine mould
centre punch
hammer
brass paper fasteners
galvanized wire
wire cutters
pliers
6 x 15 mm/⅝ in copper pipe connectors
rectangular can
fine beading wire or fuse (fine) wire

1 Cut off the tops and bottoms of the cans. Cut
along the side seams and open them out flat. Copy
the templates from the back of the book and cut them
out of paper. Attach them to the metal sheets with
adhesive tape, positioning them over attractive parts of
the designs, and cut around the shapes. Reverse one
hand and one shoe to make pairs. Cut out a smaller
flower shape from the flower template for the knees.

2 For the hair, cut a rectangle
from a can to the same width
and twice as long as the top of the
madeleine mould. Cut out the
centre, leaving a 2 cm/¾ in strip at
the top and down each side.

3 Cut each side piece into two
strips and curl each around a
pencil. Make three holes around
the top of the madeleine mould
with a centre punch and hammer.

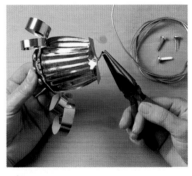

4 Fasten the hair to the
madeleine mould using paper
fasteners. Pierce a hole in the foot
of the mould and thread with a
short wire loop which will fasten
the head to the body.

5 For the bikini top, cut a slit to the centre of each flower shape. Bend the metal into a cone and fix by piercing both layers with the scissor points and inserting a paper fastener. Thread the fastened ends through a strip of metal to join the bikini top.

6 Make the skirt by cutting a rectangle of metal into a fringe. Cut a strip for the belt and cut out a buckle shape in a contrasting colour. Slot the belt through the buckle.

7 Make the arms and legs by rolling up six rectangles of can. Slot each one through a 15 mm/ ⅝ in copper pipe connector to keep the metal rolled up.

8 Cut four lengths of galvanized wire slightly longer than the arms and legs and make a hook in one end. Pierce the hands and the feet and thread one of the hooks through each hole. Twist carefully with pliers.

9 Slide a tube on to each wire, then bend the straight end of the wire into a loop.

10 Use a centre punch to make one hole in each side and two holes in the base of the rectangular can which will form the body. Thread a length of wire through the two shoulder holes, so that it protrudes from each side. Thread each end into the loops at the top of the arms, then bend into a loop and twist to secure. Cut off the excess wire.

11 Fold another length of wire in half and thread through the body can to protrude through the holes in the base. Thread the last two tubes on to these, then thread the wire through the loops on each of the lower leg sections (see Diagram 1 below). Twist the wire and trim away any excess.

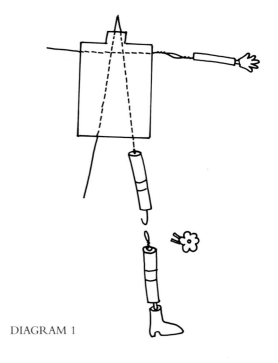

12 Pierce the kneecap flowers with a paper fastener and secure through the wire loop on each leg. Using fine wire, attach the clothing and fix the body to the wire loop on the head.

DIAGRAM 1

LEAF CURTAIN-EDGING

These stylized leaves add a finishing flourish to a stylish, airy curtain, which will shimmer in the light as the curtain shifts in the slightest breeze. Add them to ready-made fabric panels, or make your own curtains out of a softly coloured muslin.

YOU WILL NEED
tracing paper
pencil
paper
0.1 mm/¹⁄₂₅₀ in aluminium foil
protective pad
dried-out ball-point pen
small, pointed scissors
sheer curtain
tape measure
pins
glass and glitter buttons
sewing needle and matching thread
scrap wood or card (cardboard)
glue gun

1 Trace the five leaf motifs at the back of the book and transfer to plain paper to make templates. Place each template on a square of aluminium foil. Rest the foil on a protective pad and draw over the design with a dried-out ball-point pen to transfer it.

2 Turn the foil over and use scissors to cut out each leaf about 3 mm/⅛ in from the edge of the embossed outline. ▶

3 Measure and mark the positions of the buttons on the curtain. The bottom row starts 20 cm/8 in above the hem, and the buttons are placed 15 cm/6 in apart. Mark each place with a pin.

4 Sew on the buttons at the marked positions using matching thread, alternating the position of the different button designs.

5 Arrange the foil leaves, equally spaced, along the bottom of the curtain.

6 Lay the curtain on a piece of scrap wood or card and use a glue gun to stick each leaf in place.

METAL MOSAIC

Small patisserie (baking) tins come in delicate, fluted shapes that are really too pretty just to bake with. Using them in a mosaic will make you look at them in a new light. As tinware rusts easily, don't place this decoration in a damp or steamy environment.

YOU WILL NEED
8 barquette tins, 6 cm/2½ in long
fluted petit four tin, 3 cm/1¼ in diameter
biscuit (cookie) tin lid
spatula or small trowel
ready-mixed tile adhesive
diamond-shaped and circular mirror mosaic pieces
cloth
cotton buds (swabs)
strong glue
coloured glass pebble

1 Arrange small patisserie (baking) tins inside the lid of a biscuit (cookie) tin until you have a design that you like.

2 Remove the small tins and use a spatula or small trowel to spread an even layer of tile adhesive in the lid. Press the tins into position and leave to dry.

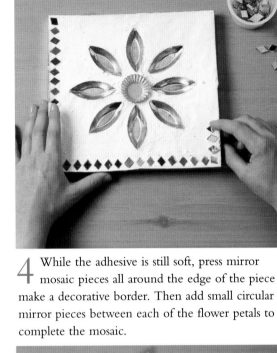

3 Add a second layer of adhesive, filling the lid to the level of the tin rims, and smooth the surface (it may help to wet the surface slightly).

4 While the adhesive is still soft, press mirror mosaic pieces all around the edge of the piece to make a decorative border. Then add small circular mirror pieces between each of the flower petals to complete the mosaic.

5 Wipe the surfaces clean with a damp cloth or damp cotton buds (swabs). Leave to harden.

6 Glue a coloured glass pebble into the tin in the centre to add focus to the design.

MEXICAN MIRROR

Inspired by Mexican folk art, this brilliantly painted and punched mirror frame
is designed to co-ordinate with the equally colourful Fiesta Chandelier. In combination,
they will give your room a touch of exotic colour and warmth.

YOU WILL NEED

paper	paintbrush
scissors	permanent felt-tip pens or
aluminium sheet	glass paints: turquoise, green,
glue stick	orange and pink
permanent marker	15 cm/6 in circular mirror
protective pad	25 cm/10 in circular cake board
hammer	double-sided adhesive pads
small and large centre	nail or fine drill bit
punches	wire cutters
protective gloves	galvanized wire
tin snips (shears or clippers)	pliers
chisel	7 short screws
blue glass paint	screwdriver

1 Enlarge the template at the back of the book to a diameter of 30 cm/12 in and then cut it out. Stick the paper pattern to the aluminium sheet using a glue stick, and trace around this carefully with a permanent marker.

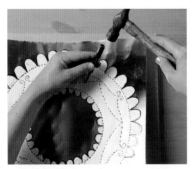

2 With the aluminium sheet resting on a protective pad, make indentations using a hammer and small centre punch along the lines of the pattern. Just two taps of the hammer at each point should be sufficient.

3 Cut out the shape using tin snips (shears or clippers); wear gloves to protect your hands. To cut out the central area, first punch a hole through the centre using a chisel, and cut from there.

4 Hammer indentations at random with a centre punch all over the inner section of the frame to give it an overall texture.

5 Paint the indented section using translucent blue glass paint. Leave to dry.

6 Colour the rest of the frame as shown using permanent felt-tip pens or glass paints.

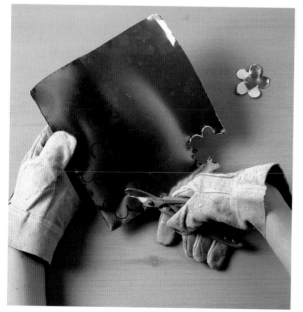

7 Draw a five petal flower template with a 5 cm/ 2 in diameter. Trace around it on an aluminium sheet with a permanent marker making seven flowers. Cut them out using tin snips (shears or clippers).

8 Colour the individual flowers using permanent felt-tip pens or glass paints.

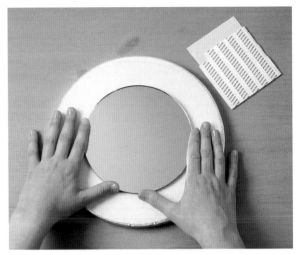

9 Place the flowers on a protective pad and use a large centre punch to hammer a hole through the centre of each one, large enough for a screw to pass through. If the flowers buckle, bend them back into shape. Make similar holes at the indented points on the frame, following the template.

10 Attach the mirror to the bottom of the cake board using double-sided adhesive pads.

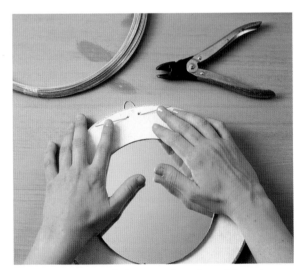

11 Pierce two holes near the edge of the cake board using a nail or fine drill bit. Cut a short piece of galvanized wire and bend into a loop to make a hanger. Thread the ends through the holes and bend flat against the board.

12 Place the frame over the mirror and backing board. Place the flowers in position so that their holes correspond with those in the frame and screw them on through the frame into the backing board. Colour the screws to match the flower centres.

PUNCHED-PANEL WALL CABINET

Tin-panelled furniture gives a clean, modern look, and this simple flower motif in aluminium will invest a room with new energy. Transform a bathroom cabinet or small cupboard by removing the centre panel from the door and replacing it with a punched-aluminium panel.

YOU WILL NEED

small wooden cabinet with panelled door
ruler
pencil
aluminium sheet
protective gloves
tin snips (shears or clippers)
paper
adhesive tape
protective pad
centre punch
hammer
panel pins (brads)

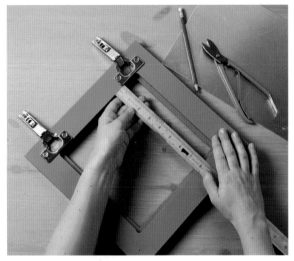

1 Remove the central panel from the cabinet door and measure the rebated area to establish the size of the metal panel.

2 Transfer the measurements to the aluminium and cut using tin snips (shears or clippers). ▶

3 Trace around the metal panel on a sheet of paper, then draw your design – in this case, a symmetrical flower.

4 Tape the paper pattern securely to the metal panel. Working on a protective pad, punch around the outlines of the design using a centre punch and hammer.

5 Remove the paper pattern, turn the panel over and punch from the other side to "raise" a section of the design: in this case, the centre of the flower. Work from the outside to the centre.

6 Fix the panel into the door by tapping a panel pin (brad) into each corner of the frame on the inside, taking care not to mark the metal. Neaten the inside by applying tape around the edge of the panel.

STYLISH SUITCASE

Turn an ordinary biscuit (cookie) tin into a stylish suitcase with webbing straps and a smart handle. You could further embellish the case by attaching a copper or aluminium foil plaque embossed with your name or initials.

YOU WILL NEED
metal drawer or cupboard handle
rectangular metal tin with hinged lid
permanent marker
drill
ruler
small nuts and bolts (or rivets)
spanner (or pop riveter)
screwdriver
narrow luggage straps
scissors
hole punch or bradawl

1 Centre the handle on the side of the tin opposite the hinges and mark the fixing positions using a permanent marker.

2 Before drilling the holes for attaching the handles, first of all ensure that the case is securely clamped (see Basic Techniques).

3 Drill handle holes as shown. Mark and drill two strap holes midway between the box sides and the handle fixings. Drill two holes in corresponding positions on the hinge (back) side of the tin case. ▶

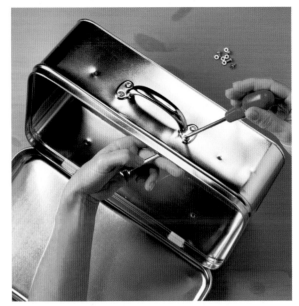

4 Attach the handle with small nuts and bolts
(or you could use rivets).

5 Cut two strips of webbing to fit around the box
and mark them with the positions of the drilled
holes. Punch a small hole at each marked point and
attach the straps in the same way as the handle.

CHRISTMAS BIRDS

Inspired by European folk art motifs, these foil birds make pretty ornaments to hang on the Christmas tree, where the embossed decorations will catch the light as they twirl. Traditional designs work particularly well with this medium.

YOU WILL NEED
tracing paper
pencil
paper
small, pointed scissors
0.1 mm/¹⁄₂₅₀ in aluminium foil
adhesive tape
protective pad
dried-out ball-point pen
dressmaker's tracing wheel
6 mm/¼ in and 3 mm/⅛ in hole punches

1 Trace and transfer the bird templates from the back of the book and cut them out of paper. Lay the templates on the aluminium foil and secure with adhesive tape. Lay the foil on a protective pad and draw around the shapes firmly using a dried-out ball-point pen.

2 Remove the templates. Draw in the top of the head and the beak of each bird with the ball-point pen. Use a dressmaker's tracing wheel to mark the dotted lines on the body, tail, neck and crown, following the guidelines on the templates.

3 Draw in the eye and the large dots on the wing and neck using the ball-point pen. Cut out the bird shapes using small, pointed scissors, cutting just outside the indented outline.

4 Make the hole for the eye with a 6 mm/¼ in hole punch, then use a small punch to make a hole in the bird's back for hanging.

BEER-CAN CANDLE SCONCE

Drinks (soda) cans are easy to recycle into attractive and useful objects such as this sconce.
The shiny interior makes an effective reflector for the candle flame, while the exterior
can be painted or left as it is if it has a pretty printed design.

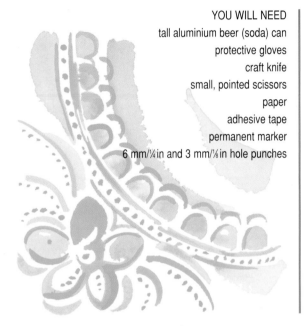

YOU WILL NEED
tall aluminium beer (soda) can
protective gloves
craft knife
small, pointed scissors
paper
adhesive tape
permanent marker
6 mm/¼ in and 3 mm/⅛ in hole punches

1 To cut the top off the can, first make a slit in the metal using a craft knife, then cut through the slit with scissors. Enlarge the template at the back of the book to fit your can, and cut it out of paper. Wrap it around the can and secure with adhesive tape. Draw around the shape using a marker pen.

2 Remove the paper template and cut around the design using small, pointed scissors. Make a short slit between each scallop.

3 Use the larger punch to make a hanging hole at the top, a hole on either side of the heart shape, and one in each scallop. Use the smaller punch to make a border all round the heart shape.

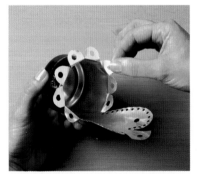

4 Fold over each scallop shape to form a decorative rim for the candle sconce.

SHIMMERING TEMPLE

*A Hindu temple was the inspiration for this charming little ornamental shrine
assembled from an assortment of tins. Hang it amongst the branches of a tree in your garden,
but keep it out of reach of children as it has sharp edges.*

YOU WILL NEED
tin cans in assorted sizes
can opener
protective gloves
tin snips (shears or clippers)
mallet
pencil
hole punch
wood block
drill
pop riveter and rivets
pliers
scrap of metal lawn-edging
(optional)
galvanized wire
wire cutters
protective pad
centre punch
hammer
3 fluted petit four tins in
different sizes

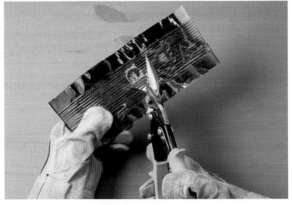

1 Remove the lids and bottoms from two cans,
using a can opener that takes off the reinforced
rims. Wash and dry them thoroughly. Cut the cans
open with tin snips and flatten with a mallet.

2 Mark windows and a door-
way on a can. Pierce with a
hole punch, working on a piece
of scrap wood. Cut out the
shapes with tin snips. Fold each
side over a block of wood and
hammer with a mallet. The
centre panel should be as wide as
the diameter of the can that will
be inside the box you are making.

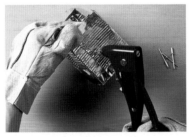

3 Repeat with the second can,
this time omitting the doors
and windows. Drill holes through
the side panels of both sections
and pop rivet together.

4 Cut a rectangle from another
flattened can, slightly larger
than the box you have made.
Turn down all four sides with
pliers, snipping the corners with
the tin snips (shears or clippers) to
form a lid.

5 Remove the lids, but not the bottoms, from two smaller cans (use two with different proportions). Mark out windows, pierce and cut as before, making sure the closed end is at the top.

6 Cut a cuff from a piece of flattened can and scallop the edge. Bend into a circle slightly larger than one of the small tins and pop rivet together.

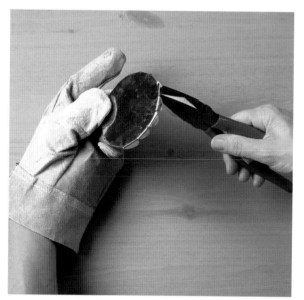

7 Cut a circle from a flattened can or large lid. Scallop the edge all round using tin snips. Fold down each scallop with pliers.

8 Make a base from a scrap of lawn-edging or a large flattened can. Fold up the side edges with pliers. Cut a long piece of galvanized wire and bend the end into a loop.

9 On a protective pad, centre punch a hole through the centre of all the various components, including the three petit four tins for the roof.

10 Now assemble the house. Starting with the base, thread the wire through all the sections. Diagram 1 below shows an alternative threading order to the final photograph.

DIAGRAM 1

11 When you reach the top of the tin construction, trim away any excess wire and bend the top into a hook for hanging.

METAL-FACED DRAWERS

Whether you want to jazz up an old piece of furniture or add panache to a new,
plain chest of drawers, corrugated metal lawn-edging is perfect for the job. Simply find
the most suitable width, cut it to size and screw it to the drawer fronts.

YOU WILL NEED
tape measure
set of drawers
metal lawn-edging strip
tin snips (shears or clippers)
protective gloves
scrap board
drill
permanent marker
screws
screwdriver
drawer handles or knobs

1 Measure the drawer fronts and cut the lawn-
edging to size using tin snips (shears or clippers).

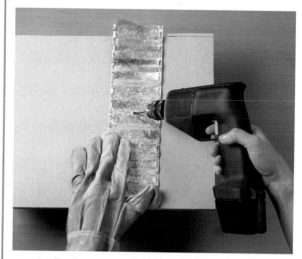

2 Drill a hole in each corner of the metal strips
and in the centre for the handle. Note clamping ▶
instructions outlined on page 86 (not shown here).

3 Lay the metal on the front of the drawer and mark the positions of the drilled holes.

4 Drill the four corners of the drawer front. Follow the safety instructions in Basic Techniques.

5 Using the four drilled holes, screw the metal strip to the drawer front.

6 Finally, attach a decorative handle to the centre front of each drawer.

STRING DISPENSER

This ingenious accessory for your workshop or garden shed efficiently dispenses different kinds of string from its three funnels. Collect interesting printed tins to recycle into a brilliant patchwork background that can be hung on the wall.

YOU WILL NEED
assorted printed tin cans
can opener
protective gloves
tin snips (shears or clippers)
mallet
protective pad
length of wood, 10 x 2 cm/4 x ¾ in
nails
hammer
ruler
3 metal funnels
permanent marker
drill
2 mirror fixing plates
screws
screwdriver
3 balls of string

1 Take the lids and bottoms off the cans using a can opener that removes the reinforced rims and wash and let dry. Cut the cans open with tin snips and flatten them out using a mallet. Over a protective pad, select two flat cans slightly wider than the wood and nail them to each end so that they overlap the edges.

2 Snip the corners of the tins so that they can be folded over the edges of the wood. Hammer the edges down with the mallet, then nail to secure.

3 Lay the other cans along the wood until you are happy with the arrangement. Nail them down to cover the wood completely, overlapping them slightly. Fold over the edges as before and nail to secure.

4 Measure the finished panel and establish the positions for the funnels. Mark with a permanent marker. Drill a guide hole at each marked point. Turn the panel over and attach two mirror fixing plates at the back for hanging. ▶

5 Drill a hole in exactly the same position in each of the funnels and screw them into the guide holes on the panel.

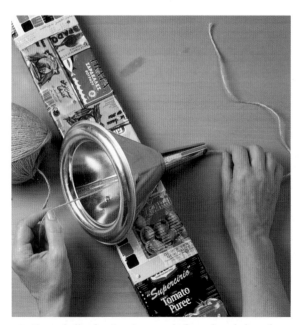

6 Put a ball of string into each funnel and thread the end (taken from the centre of the ball) through the spout.

FIESTA CHANDELIER

This flamboyant chandelier has been created using patisserie (baking) tins and other baking accessories, which come in a wide range of useful shapes and sizes to inspire you. Add rich tropical colours with glass paints and permanent felt-tip pens.

YOU WILL NEED

30 cm/12 in diameter fluted flan ring, 2.5 cm/1 in deep
permanent marker pen
galvanized wire
wire cutters
round-nosed pliers
blue glass paint
paintbrush
permanent felt-tip pens: turquoise, green, pink and orange
9 fluted petit four tins
protective pad
hammer
2.5 cm/1 in galvanized nails
centre punch (optional)
paper
pencil
scissors
aluminium sheet
protective gloves
tin snips (shears or clippers)
chisel-ended bradawl
brass paper fasteners
strong glue
glass pebbles
3 wired glass-bead necklaces or plug chains

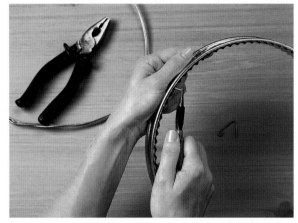

1 Count the flutings on the inner flan ring and mark off three equal sections. Cut three short pieces of wire and thread them through the ring at the marked points. Make a loop at the top of each wire using round-nosed pliers and bend the other end up inside the flan ring to secure the loop.

2 Paint the inside of the ring, and the wire loops, with blue glass paint. Leave to dry.

3 Colour the outside of the ring with turquoise and green permanent felt-tip pens.

4 Place the petit four tins on a protective pad and use a hammer and nail or centre punch to drive a hole through the centre of each tin.

5 Colour the petit four tins orange with a permanent felt-tip pen. Then mark nine equally spaced points on the ring for the candleholders. Press a nail through the centre of each of the petit four tins and insert in the ring – it should fit snugly in the flutes of the ring.

6 Draw a flower template with a 5 cm/2 in diameter and use it to draw nine flowers on the aluminium sheet. Cut out using tin snips (shears or clippers).

7 Cut one more aluminium flower, twice the size of the others, then colour all the flowers using permanent felt-tip pens.

8 Using a chisel-ended bradawl, cut a slit in the centre of each of the flowers.

9 Slot a brass paper fastener through the centre of each flower. (Check the size of an opened fastener against the outside of the flan ring – you may need to trim the tips.)

10 Fix on the flowers by sliding the opened tips of the paper fasteners under the rolled rims of the flan ring in between the candleholders. Add a spot of strong glue to hold them securely.

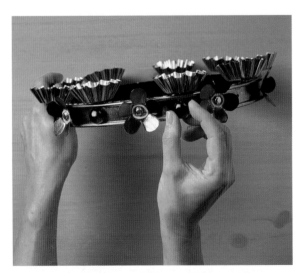

11 Glue the glass pebbles to the ring midway between the flowers.

12 Thread a length of wire through the large flower and bend it into a hanging loop at the top and a hook beneath the flower. Attach three chains to the loops on the ring and suspend them from the hook. If you are using necklaces, make sure they are strong enough to take the weight, and colour the glass beads to match the chandelier.

MOORISH FLOWER BLIND

This lightweight blind is constructed from bold floral shapes with a geometric precision that is reminiscent of Islamic decorative motifs. It is easy to hang, but use it at a high window, out of children's reach, as the metal edges are sharp.

YOU WILL NEED
protective gloves
scissors
heavy-duty aluminium foil pie dishes
paper
pencil
scrap wood
bradawl
round-nosed pliers
jewellery jump rings (wires)

1 Wearing gloves to protect your hands, cut the rim from a heavy-duty aluminium foil pie dish.

2 Enlarge the template at the back of the book to the same diameter as the pie dish base and cut it out. Place the template centrally on the foil disc and trace around it. Cut out the foil shape. Repeat to make as many flowers as you need for your blind.

3 Cut some of the flower shapes in half to make straight-sided pieces for the edges of the blind.

4 Cut one flower shape in quarters to form the four corners of the blind.

5 Lay out the flowers on a piece of scrap wood. Using a bradawl, pierce a hole about 3 mm/⅛ in from the end of each strut between the flower petals.

6 Using round-nosed pliers, open as many jump rings (wires) as you need to join the flowers. Hook a ring through the hole in one strut, and join it to the hole in an adjacent flower. Close the ring. Repeat with all the flowers.

7 Add the side and corner pieces to complete the blind. Add a row of jump rings (wires) along the top of the blind from which to hang it.

TREETOP ANGEL

Adapted from the simple paper angels that we all made as children, this embossed pewter design will add a touch of elegance to the top of your Christmas tree. If you wish, you can use permanent felt-tip pens to enliven it with colour.

YOU WILL NEED
pencil
paper
masking tape
pewter shim
protective pad
dressmaker's tracing wheel
dried-out ball-point pen
pinking shears
craft knife
permanent marker

1 Enlarge the template at the back of the book to the size you require. Tape the paper template to the pewter shim. Lay the sheet on a protective pad and use a dressmaker's tracing wheel to trace over the double outlines.

2 Draw over all the solid lines using a dried-out ball-point pen. Indent the dots using a pencil.

3 Cut around the shape using pinking shears. Be particularly careful when cutting around the halo and wing tips. If you bend some of the zigzag edging, smooth it back into shape with your fingers.

4 Turn the angel over. Following the paper pattern, complete the remaining embossed markings from the reverse side, pressing in dots for the eyes and at the centre point of each star.

5 Use a craft knife to cut a slit around the head, inside the halo. Be careful not to cut too near the neck so as not to weaken it. Cut the two slits beside the wings where marked.

6 Roll the head and neck slightly around a cylindrical object such as a marker.

7 Bend the angel's body into a curve and slot together as shown.

CLASSIC MAILBOX

Fix this traditionally styled mailbox to your garden gate with its door open and the reflective indicator will tell you at a glance when the door is closed and your post has arrived.
The smart metal cladding is cut from a large cooking-oil can.

YOU WILL NEED

pencil	screws
2 cm/¾ in exterior plywood	2 cranked brass hinges
tenon saw	(spring hinges)
saucer or plate	protective gloves
coping-saw, jigsaw or	tin snips (shears or clippers)
band-saw	cooking-oil drum
sandpaper	metal straight edge
tinted exterior varnish	scrap wood
(or polyurethane)	mallet
paintbrush	drill
nails	bicycle reflective indicator
hammer	bolt
	spanner (wrench)

1 Following the templates at the back of the book, mark the dimensions of the mailbox base, back and door on the plywood surface and cut out. By tracing round a saucer or plate, mark the curves on the back and door.

2 Cut out the curved shapes using a coping-saw, jigsaw or band-saw. Smooth all the sawn edges with sandpaper.

3 Paint all the wooden pieces with tinted exterior varnish (or polyurethane) and leave to dry.

4 Hammer nails into the back section then hammer the back on to the base section.

5 Screw the hinges to the door and attach to the front of the wooden base.

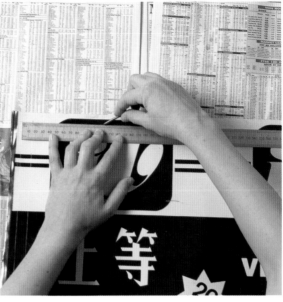

6 Use tin snips (shears or clippers) to cut off the top and bottom of the oil can. Cut down the seam and lay out flat. Using the template measurements, mark the metal using a straight edge and nail.

7 Cut out the metal sheet using tin snips (shears or clippers), wearing gloves to protect your hands.

8 Cut out the small rectangle marked at each of the corners.

▶

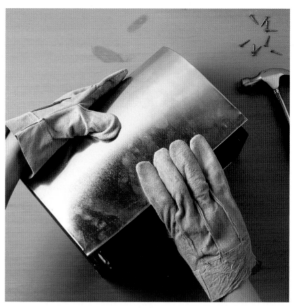

9 Protecting the work surface with some scrap wood, turn in the edges of the metal to eliminate the sharp edges. Tap them flat with a mallet.

10 Pull the metal cover over the wooden base, aligning the edges.

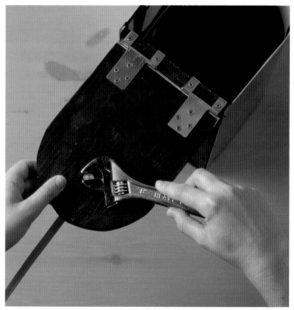

11 Nail the metal to the base and back, starting at the centre of each side and working out. Remember to keep the door free.

12 Drill a hole through the door for the indicator and fix in place with a bolt.

HAMMERED WEATHER VANE

You don't need metal-working skills to make this cheerful and effective weather vane,
as the shapes are cut out of rigid plastic sheet covered with roof-flashing which is then given a
hammered texture. Set the arrow to indicate north.

YOU WILL NEED

paper
scissors
permanent marker pen
rigid plastic sheet (Plexiglas)
coping-saw, jigsaw or
band-saw
scrap wood
drill
craft knife
small paint roller
galvanized wire
self-adhesive aluminium
roof-flashing
metal straight edge
hack-saw
file
brass screw
screwdriver
metal rod or broom handle
newspaper
small hammer
blue glass paint
paintbrush

1 Scale up the template at the back of the book and cut out paper patterns of the cockerel (rooster) and an arrow 24 cm (9½ in) long. Draw around these marking the shapes on the plastic sheet.

2 Cut out the shapes using a coping-saw, jigsaw or band-saw. Using a piece of scrap wood to protect your work surface, drill a row of small holes as shown. Drill a hole for the cockerel's eye.

3 Use a craft knife to cut the central plastic tube from a small paint roller and use galvanized wire to attach it to the cockerel shape.

4 Cut strips of aluminium roof-flashing long enough to cover the plastic shapes. Trim the edges of the strips using a craft knife and straight edge, so that you will be able to make neat joints.

5 Apply the strips of flashing to both sides of the cockerel, trimming around the edges as you stick them on. Wrap the lower strips on the cockerel around the roller.

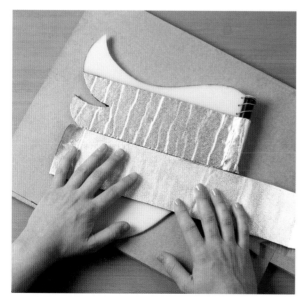

6 As you apply further strips, butt the long edges carefully together. Cut out the eye of the cockerel. Cover the arrow in the same way and drill a small hole for the screw.

7 Using a hack-saw, cut off the bent section of the paint roller handle. File the sawn edges smooth.

▶

8 Screw the arrow to the plastic roller handle. Fit the roller handle to the metal rod or broom handle to make a mount for the weather vane.

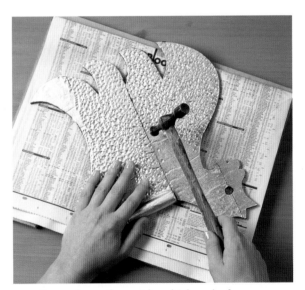

9 Cover the surface with a thick pad of newspaper. With a small hammer, tap gently all over both sides of the bird to give it texture. Colour the area marked on the template using blue glass paint. Erect the weather vane with the arrow pointing north.

MATERIALS

ALUMINIUM ROOF-FLASHING
This simple and adaptable material has a self-adhesive backing and comes in various different widths and finishes.

ALUMINIUM SHEET
Large sheets can be cut to size using tin snips (shears or clippers). Use this for large projects such as door panels. Large cooking-oil cans (drums) are also a good source of large sheet aluminium.

BISCUIT (COOKIE) TINS
Both tins and lids provide sturdy pieces of flat tinned steel.

DOUBLE-SIDED CARPET TAPE
This heavy-duty adhesive tape is useful for attaching foil motifs to card or board.

FOIL
Aluminium or copper foil is suitable for making small embossed motifs. It is thicker and stronger than baking foil and will not rip, but is thin enough to cut easily with scissors.

FOOD AND DRINKS (SODA) CANS
Aluminium and tinned-steel cans are a good source of sheet metal. Aluminium drinks (soda) cans can be cut with scissors, while food cans require tin snips (shears or clippers). Colourful printed cans can be found in delicatessens or ethnic food stores.

METAL LAWN-EDGING
This slightly corrugated metal strip is available from garden centres and hardware shops in several widths.

NAILS, SCREWS AND WASHERS
These can be used functionally and decoratively: look in hardware shops for interesting shapes.

PAINTS AND PENS
Translucent colour can be used on metal, permanent felt-tip pens and glass paints are particularly good.

PATISSERIE (BAKING) ACCESSORIES
Cake tins, moulds and rings are made in a fantastic variety of shapes and sizes.

SHIM
Thicker than foil, this can be cut with scissors. Available in pewter, copper, aluminium and brass.

WIRE
For binding components together and for making hanging hooks, use galvanized garden wire. Fine beading wire and fuse (fine) wire may be suitable for small pieces.

Opposite, clockwise from top left: Aluminium drinks (soda) and food cans; cake mould ring; roof-flashing; biscuit tin; permanent felt-tip pens; garden edging; wire; aluminium sheet; nails; small cake tins; screws and washers; double-sided carpet tape; fuse (fine) wire; rolls of foil and shim.

EQUIPMENT

CENTRE PUNCH AND HAMMER
Use for punching holes in metal sheet. A large strong nail or bradawl can be used instead.

DRESSMAKER'S TRACING WHEEL
This will indent perfect regular dotted lines in foil or shim.

DRILL
For drilling holes in preparation for bolting, riveting, nailing or screwing metal components.

EMBOSSING TOOLS
Almost any pointed object can be used as an embossing tool. A double-ended embossing stylus has large and small heads for broad and fine indentations. A dried-out ball-point pen is excellent as it glides well over the metal. For broad strokes use a lollipop (Popsicle) stick or skewer; for fine ones use the blunt end of a needle.

HOLE PUNCH
Designed for use on paper, this will also work on metal foil.

MALLET
This is useful for straightening and flattening pieces of metal sheet.

PLIERS
For bending metal and wire.

POP RIVETER
This tool enables you to join two pieces of drilled metal together.

PROTECTIVE GLOVES
It is advisable to wear these when working with sharp sheet metal.

PROTECTIVE PADS
When punching holes in metal, work on a surface that is firm but yielding. Use a plastic pad, a rubber or composition (cutting) mat or a sheet of thick cardboard (card stock). A foam mat is an ideal surface when embossing foil or shim.

RULER
A metal straight edge is used for embossing straight lines.

SCISSORS
Household scissors will cut through aluminium drinks (soda) cans, foil and shim. Use small, pointed scissors, such as embroidery scissors, for cutting out delicate shapes in foil. Pinking shears will produce a decorative edge.

TIN SNIPS (SHEARS OR CLIPPERS)
For cutting sheets of metal or food cans. Shears are used for heavier-gauge metal sheet. Wear protective gloves when using snips or shears.

Opposite, clockwise from top left: Protective gloves; protective pad; pop riveter with rivets; shears; bradawl; embossing stylus; scissors; pliers; drill; tin snips; a selection of pliers; hammer; mallet; tin opener.
Opposite, centre: Dressmaker's tracing wheel; steel ruler; centre punch.

BASIC TECHNIQUES

When working with tin it is important to familiarize yourself with the basic techniques relating both to the different kinds of tin available and to the required effects. The following methods show how to work with tin with maximum safety, as well as featuring decorative techniques for tin used throughout the projects such as indenting, punching and colouring.

CUTTING METAL

There are a number of different techniques for cutting metal, depending on what sort of tin you are using. Remember to wear protective gloves when working with sharp metal edges.

ALUMINIUM DRINKS (SODA) CANS

Drinks (soda) cans are generally made of thin aluminium which can easily be cut with scissors.

STEEL FOOD CANS

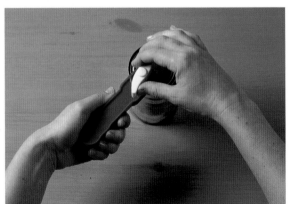

1 Remove the tops of food cans with an opener that cuts into the can's side, removing the rim.

2 Wearing protective gloves, use tin snips (shears or clippers) to cut along the side seam of the can.

SQUARE BISCUIT (COOKIE) TINS

1 A biscuit (cookie) tin is a good source of flat, strong sheet metal. Cut down the corners using tin snips (shears or clippers).

2 Cut off the side panels along the inside of the bottom rim.

3 Remove the side panels, leaving a square of flat metal.

LARGE COOKING-OIL CANS

1 To flatten a cooking-oil can, cut initially with a hack-saw.

2 Cut around the rims with tin snips (shears or clippers). Then cut down the side seam. Degrease the metal thoroughly before use.

CUTTING ENCLOSED AREAS

1 To cut into an enclosed area, you first need to make a hole large enough to insert tin snips (shears or clippers). Use a hammer and chisel to punch a slit.

2 Insert the tin snips and enlarge the central hole sufficiently to allow you to direct the snips into the angles of the cut-out shape

CUTTING FANCY SHAPES

1 Use small tin snips (shears or clippers) for tricky shapes such as these flowers. Start by cutting slots between the petals. Get a smoother cut by not allowing the blades to meet completely.

2 Next, cut from the top of the petal to the base of the previous cut. Work all the way round cutting each petal halfway.

3 Then work in the opposite direction to complete.

OTHER TECHNIQUES

FLATTENING METAL

A mallet is ideal for this purpose. Wearing gloves to protect your hands, lay the metal on a piece of scrap wood and hammer it evenly all over. If you have to use an ordinary hammer, lay a sheet of hardboard over the metal sheet and hammer over that.

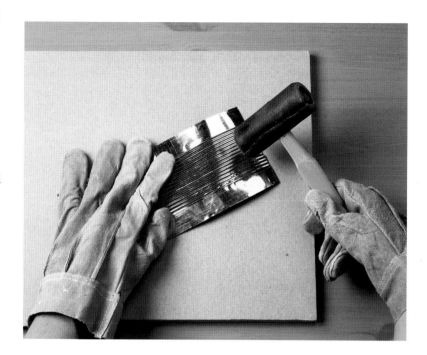

NEATENING EDGES

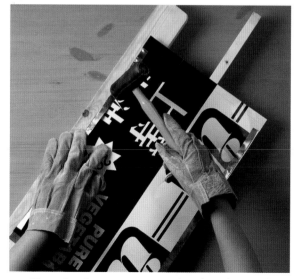

1 Clamp a straight-sided block of wood firmly in a bench vice. Draw a 1 cm/½ in border along the edge of the sheet, align it with the edge of the wood and hold steady with a second piece of wood. Use a mallet to fold the metal over the edge of the block.

2 Turn the sheet over, supporting the edge on the wooden block. Hammer the folded edge flat.

DRILLING METAL

1 Tape small objects to a larger block of wood which can be clamped to the work bench. Masking tape will also help to stop the drill slipping.

2 For drilling into a can or any small, hollow object, insert a piece of wood, clamp it to the bench and the can to the wood. If it is a delicate item, insert offcuts of leather between the metal and the clamp to protect it.

3 When drilling a large hollow item, ensure that the surface you are drilling is supported to prevent it buckling. Clamp a piece of wood to the inside, then secure the whole object to the work bench.

As the steps above illustrate, extreme care must be taken when drilling metal, especially if it has sharp edges. The metal must be secured to prevent it spinning on the drill bit. It should always be clamped: never hold the metal in your hand when drilling it. Wear safety goggles and protective gloves. First make an indentation using a centre punch to guide the drill, then hold the drill directly over the surface and do not apply too much pressure as it will cause distortion and may result in the drill slipping.

When drilling through small or three-dimensional objects it is necessary to use a work bench and clamps.

RIVETING

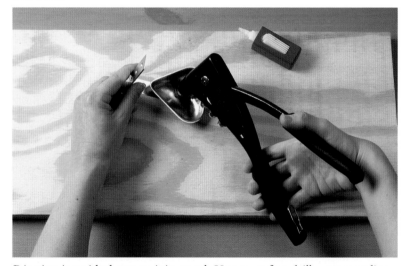

Riveting is an ideal way to join metal. You must first drill corresponding holes in the two surfaces. Use the correct sized rivet – it must be a tight fit in the hole – and ensure that the two surfaces are tightly pressed together. It may help to use glue or tape to hold them temporarily. Squeeze the handles of the riveter until you hear the "pop".

DECORATIVE TECHNIQUES

INDENTING FOIL

It is easy to impress a pattern in foil or shim. It can be done freehand using a ball-point pen, or using a dressmaker's tracing wheel or even a pastry edger. Work on a surface that is firm but yielding, such as a foam mat.

PUNCHING METAL

Use a hammer and centre punch, or even a nail. If holding either becomes hard on your fingers, use a pair of pliers. Two taps with the hammer will be sufficient for an indented pattern; if you want to pierce the metal, use greater force.

USING STENCILS AND TEMPLATES

Draw or trace a pattern on paper and attach it to the metal sheet using a glue stick. The metal can be kept steady by attaching it to a piece of chipboard with panel pins (tacks). When you remove the template, wash the glue off the metal with warm soapy water.

COLOURING

Translucent colour works best on tinware, as it does not obscure the metallic look: use glass paints and permanent felt-tip pens. The metal surface must be clean and grease-free. Mistakes can be removed with cotton wool (balls) and turpentine. As it is difficult to get an even coverage with transparent colours, they work best on a textured background. Use short, even strokes when using felt tips to enhance the texture.

TEMPLATES

Where no measurements or enlargements are given, the templates are shown at the same size. Enlarge on a photocopier, or trace the design and draw a grid of evenly spaced squares on your tracing. Draw a larger grid on to another piece of paper and copy the outline square by square.

Repoussé Frame, pp. 19–21

Christmas Birds, pp. 46–47
Enlarge by 125% for actual size.

Embossed Greetings Cards, pp. 16–18

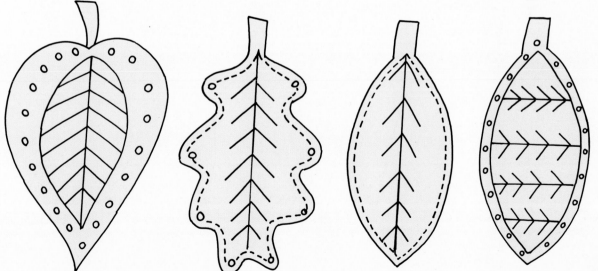

Beer-can Candle Sconce, pp. 48–49. Enlarge by 125% for actual size.

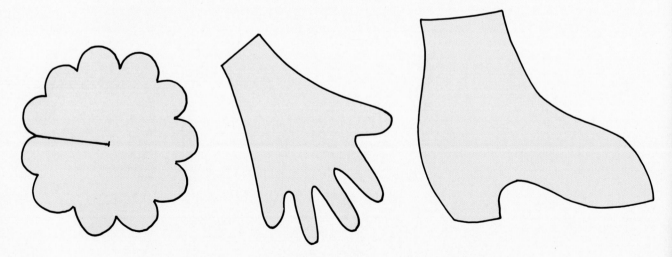

Musical Scarecrow, pp. 26–29. Enlarge by 125% for actual size.

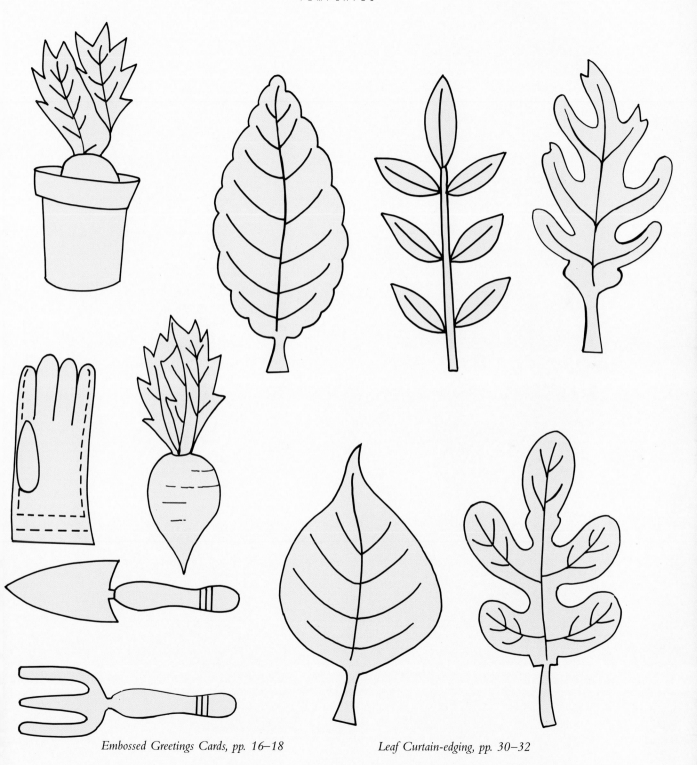

Embossed Greetings Cards, pp. 16–18　　　　*Leaf Curtain-edging, pp. 30–32*

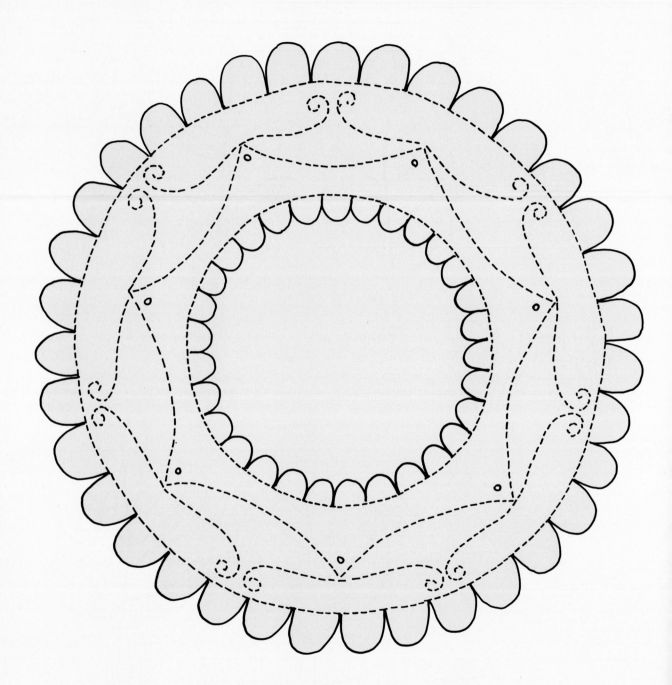

Mexican Mirror, pp. 36–39. Enlarge by 200% for actual size.

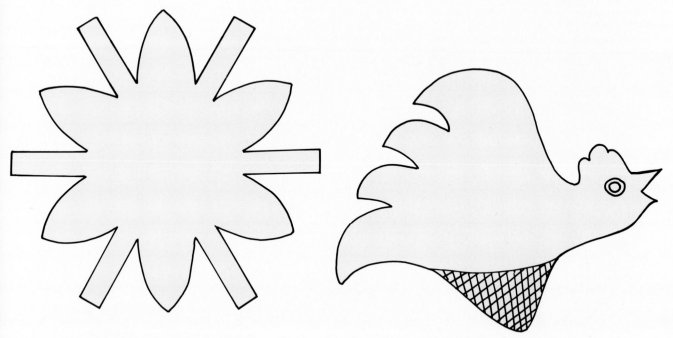

Moorish Flower Blind, pp. 64–66
Enlarge by 200% for actual size.

Hammered Weather Vane, pp. 74–77
Enlarge by 300% for actual size.

Scrollwork Doorstop, pp 22–25
Use this template as a guide to draw the lines freehand.

Treetop Angel, pp. 67–69. Enlarge by 200% for actual size.

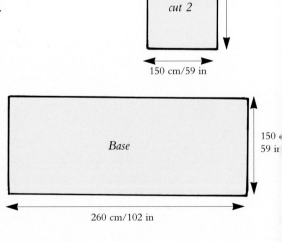

Back and door sections, cut 2

200 cm/ 79 in

150 cm/59 in

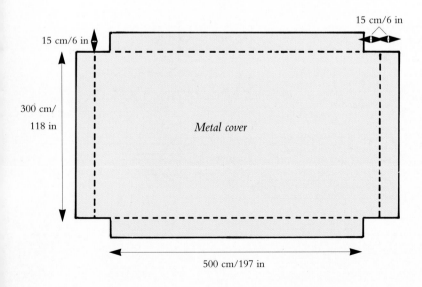

15 cm/6 in

15 cm/6 in

300 cm/ 118 in

Metal cover

500 cm/197 in

Base

150 cm/ 59 in

260 cm/102 in

Classic Mailbox, pp. 70–73

SUPPLIERS

Most equipment can be bought from well-stocked hardware shops. Recycled tin and metal foils can be bought in large craft shops.

UNITED KINGDOM

Blade Runner
Neal's Yard, Covent Garden
London WC2H 9DP
Tel: 0171 379 7391
Metal Stencils

Buck and Ryan
Tottenham Court Road
London W1V 0DY
Tel: 0171 636 7475
Tools and equipment for metalwork

Bude Time Enterprises Ltd
Higher Wharf, Bude
Cornwall EX23 8LW
Tel: 01288 342832
Clock mechanisms

Divertimenti
139-141 Fulham Road
London SW3 6HH
Tel: 0171 581 8065
Food moulds

Clay Brothers Metal Suppliers
The Green, High Street, Ealing
London W5 5DA
Tel: 0181 567 2215
Sheet metal suppliers

Southern Handicrafts
20 Kensington Gardens
Brighton BN1 4AL
Tel: 01273 681901 *(shim)*

Alec Tiranti
Warren Street
London W1 5DG
Tel: 0171 636 8565
Foils

UNITED STATES

Charrette
P.O. Box 4010
Woburn Store
Woburn, MA 01888
Tel: (781) 935 6000 x319

Creative Craft House
P.O. Box 2567
Bullhead City, AZ 86430
Tel: (520) 754 3300

Dick Blick
P.O. Box 1267
Galesburg, IL 61402
Tel: (800) 828 4548

Metalliferous
34 West 46th Street
New York, NY 10036
Tel: (212) 944 0909

Pearl Discount Art & Craft
3756 Roswell Road
Atlanta, GA 30342
Tel: (404) 233 9400
Metal plate, foils and tools

Pearl Paint Co.
308 Canal Street
New York, NY 10013
Tel: (800) 221 6845
Paint and gilding supplies

Sax Arts and Crafts
2405 S. Calhoun Road
P.O. Box 51710
New Berlin, WI 53151
General craft supplies

Universal Wirecraft Company
P.O. Box 20206
Bradenton, FL 34203
Tel: (813) 745 1219
Wirecraft and metalwork tools

Wood-met Services
3314 Shoff Circle, Dept CSS
Peoria, IL 61604
Equipment for metalworking

CANADA

Abbey Arts & Crafts
Hastings Street
Burnaby, B.C.
Tel: (604) 299 5201
Metal foils and general materials

Dundee Hobby Craft
1518-6551 No 3 Road
Richmond, B.C.
Tel: (604) 278 5713
Metal foils, materials and equipment

FunCraft City Ltd
13890-104 Avenue
Surrey, B.C.
Tel: (604) 583 3262
Metal foils

Lee Valley
S.W. Marine Drive
Vancouver, B.C.
Tel: (604) 261 2262

INDEX